QUAIL FARMING

MARKETS &MARKETING STRATEGIES

'Our business in life is not to get a head of others, but to get a head of ourselves, to break our own records, to outstrip our yesterdays by today, to do our work with more force than ever before.'

Stewart Johnson

Special Dedication

I am proud to dedicate this book to every Quail bird farmer there. Specifically, this book is purposely written for that new quail bird farmer who is struggling to find working markets and marketing strategies to adopt in order to realize more profitable returns out of quail farming venture.

Disclaimer

Copyright © 2014 Francis O. All rights reserved. No part of this publication maybe reproduced, stored in a retrieval system, or transmitted in any form or by any means – electronic, mechanical, photocopy, recording, or any other – except for brief quotations in print or online reviews, without the prior permission of the author/publisher.

The writing of this material has been a humble undertaking by the author to facilitate quail farmers and other interested parties in quail farming with useful information as they go about day to day running of their quail farms.

While the author has made every effort to ensure that the information contained herein is accurate and up-to-date, you should always exercise your own independent skill and judgment when using contents herein. Always readily seek for the input of experienced poultry professionals within your area, should emergent scenarios arise from your farm.

Acknowledgements

I am most appreciative of the many people who offered their invaluable views, ideas and support towards the making of this book.

In particular, I want to thank, with lots of humility, my family members, friends and relatives for their relentless prayers and support. Thank you all and may the almighty God bless you richly

Finally, but most important, I thank God for the gift of life and for His endless blessings upon my life. Indeed, great is His faithfulness. His grace, love and mercy endure forever.

What is a quail bird?

A quail bird is described as *a kind of game bird within the family of Phasianidae*. It is smaller than a chicken and not as well known as the pigeon (*definition according to vocabulary.com*).

According to *Scripture Alphabet of Animals by Mrs. Harriet N. Cook*, a quail bird is described to be the size of a pigeon.
It is called bird of passage because it does not live in the same place. It spends winter in one country and flies away to another country in spring.
In their journeys, they fly together in very large flocks, as you have perhaps seen wild geese or pigeons do.

Well, this book focuses on domesticated quails and not on the wild quails. Nonetheless, I thought it was beneficial to paint the picture of what a quail bird is to a reader who has never encountered one.

Next, let's go through some of the most common quail farming mistakes every serious quail farmer should aim to avoid. This is vital for quail farmers who long for sustainable profitable returns from the birds.

Five common quail farming mistakes every farmer should avoid

'People who succeed have momentum. The more they succeed, the more they want to succeed, and the more they find a way to succeed. Similarly, when someone is failing, the tendency is to get on a downward spiral that can even become a self-fulfilling prophecy.'

Tony Robbins

First Mistake: Rush to make a quick-kill

'When you enchant People, your goal is not to make money from them or to get them to do what you want, but to fill them with great delight'.
Guy Kawaski

Who doesn't want to earn some quick and easy money? I guess most people would be in need of getting such fast and easy money. However, this is one area which has killed the dreams of many would be successful quail bird farmers. It is true that too much ambition can kill a man!

Truth is, quail farming can be a very lucrative venture. However, it can only be a lucrative venture to a farmer who is not only patient, but is equally willing to go the extra mile and have in place all the quail raising requisites.

Any quail bird farmer whose focus is fixed on making quick huge returns out of this venture without any relevant inputs is bound to be miserably frustrated, and must eventually fail!

Second Mistake: Purchasing of already egg-laying birds for commercial egg production

When quails begin to lay eggs, it is never easy for an inexperienced quail farmer to tell their exact ages. It is therefore, possible for an inexperienced quail farmer to purchase quails in their third years of egg laying, or quails approaching their egg-laying-menopause (if the purchase is made at the egg-laying stage).

It is very interesting to note that in terms of growth, quail birds do slow down and would eventually stop putting on more weight as their approach full maturity. Therefore, just by looking at the size of any quail bird, at times it would not be easy to tell its exact age.

It is equally proven through research that female quail birds do lay eggs consistently within their first years of egg production. However, in the subsequent years, their rate of egg production may slow down, or may become inconsistent, and eventually disappear as they age. Did you know an egg laid by a four year old quail may be infertile? This would result into massive waste of resources and time by any farmer on such quail birds, especially if he/she intends to incubate the produced eggs. .

It is recommended that for commercial quail farming, or for a more productive quail farming, especially quail bird farming for commercial egg production, a farmer should aim to purchase utmost, five weeks old quail birds. At that stage, their vitality and productiveness is highly guaranteed. However, if a farmer has the capacity to hatch quail eggs then that would be the most recommended option.

Third Mistake: Starting Quail farming without relevant approvals or permits

Did you know at one point in history, quail birds almost became extinct? Therefore, in order to preserve and increase their numbers in the world, most governments across the globe do classify quail birds as endangered wild animals. They then provide for their protection through certain legislations.

If you reside in a country where such legislations do exist then you need to do the right thing: get the relevant approvals before venturing into rearing the birds. You can never play hide and seek with the authorities forever. There is a common saying in our country, that *'the Government has long arms'*. If you however, decide to carry out this activity without relevant approvals, then it would possibly not take too long before relevant authorities catches up with you.

Fourth Mistake: Worrying about where to sell quail products even before starting quail farming.

Worrying about where to sell quail products is a common habit amongst many people who want to venture into quail farming. But then let's be realistic here. Why would you be worried of the existence or non-existence of markets to products you do not even posses in the first place? It beats any viable logic.

Generally, a number of successful and sustainable business enterprises are mostly, driven by passion, and not any anticipated huge returns. When you have passion in what you do, then the proverbial *the rest will fall in their respective places* must eventually follow. Finding a lucrative market for your quail products would not take long before being realized once you rightfully start off the venture.

Fifth Mistake: Starting the whole venture without a clear idea of what one intends to achieve.

It is usually advisable to start any serious business venture with a business a plan. However, in quail farming, one does not necessarily need to start out with a business plan, but must incorporate it along the way for long term benefits.

What do you really want to achieve out of your quail farming venture? An anonymous best put it that *When you fail to plan then you automatically plans to fail.* Lack of proper planning usually leads to several desperate acts which may eventually push any farmer to start focusing on the short term returns rather than in the long term returns.

A typical example of lack of planning and clear focus would be to start quail farming with say, over a thousand birds, and only to sell almost all the birds at throw-away prices. Then at some point again, be tempted to start rearing the birds again. If such might be your focus then stock market trading best suits you. However, even in the stock market business, the whole environment is usually unpredictable and demands for elements of patience and consistency.

Some quick facts about quails

'Best way to sell something: don't sell anything. Earn the awareness, respect, and trust of those who might buy.'

Rand Fishkin

- Quails are small in body size when compared to chickens. This makes them require minimal spaces for housing.

- Quail bird eggs are cholesterol free. This makes the eggs a favorite for consumption by persons suffering from hypertension. The birds' meat and eggs are preferred alternative sources of protein.

- Quails are resistant to a number of diseases affecting other poultry birds. They require minimal, and in most cases, no vaccinations against diseases if taken good care of.

- On average, female quails start to lay eggs at the age of six weeks. They lay an average of 25 eggs in a good month, translating to over 300 eggs in a good year (especially the Japanese quails). Thereafter, their rate of egg production may start to decline (depending on breed and care given afterwards).

- Quail chicks are very sensitive to cold and hot weather. They should always be handled with extra care. However, mature quail birds are can survive in harsh environmental conditions.

- From hatching, quail chicks take between 4-6 weeks to reach maturity (depending on breed and care given during the rearing period).

- Quails' eggs are multicolored. Research has shown that consuming the eggs helps to improve fertility.

- Quails are fussy feeders. They eat small quantities of

feeds. Notably, they can be seen eating for a long time, but you should never be worried about overfeeding them. They know when to stop eating. Interestingly, they comfortably feed on commercial chicken feeds.

- Did you know there are over fifteen different breeds of quail birds?

Comparison between quail farming and chicken farming

'Take up one idea. Make that one idea your life – think of it, dream it, live on that idea. Let the brain, muscles, nerves, every part of your body, be full of that idea, and just leave every other idea alone. This is the way to success.'

Swami Vivekananda

Quail Farming

- Quail birds are smaller in body size hence, they require smaller cages (housing).

- In terms of feeds, quails do consume an equivalent of one eight of chicken feeds. They are fussy feeders.

- Most quail breeds are disease resistant. They require less attention and few or no vaccinations/treatments.

- Quail bird products, meat and eggs, are richly nutritious. These products have equally been scientifically proven to contain health and medicinal values.

- Keeping quails require less capital input, but with good returns.

- Did you know quails can be sourced from the wild? Naturally, they are wild birds hence do not need to be necessarily reared, especially for their meat. You can as well hunt them in the wild/forest.

- Quail can be conveniently transported from one place to another due to their smaller body size and lighter weight, as compared to chickens of similar ages.

- Quail bird products: chicks, eggs, and meat, fetch higher market prices as compared to similar chicken products.

Chicken Farming

- When compared to quails, chickens are naturally bigger in size and therefore, require a bigger space for housing.

- Chickens do require feeds in large quantities as compared to quails.

- Chickens are prone to many poultry-related disease infections; hence do require close and constant monitoring plus vaccinations and treatments.

- Chickens' products, meat, and eggs, are less nutritious, and with minimal health benefits. Equally, these products have less or no proven medicinal values when compared to quail bird products.

- In order to realize tangible profits, chicken farming would require more monetary input as compared to quail bird farming.

- There are no alternatives to rearing chickens. They are domestic animals, unlike quail birds which can be sourced from the wild.

- Chicken are heavy in weight and appear bigger in size when compared to quails. It is therefore, very burdensome to transport a large portion of chickens from one location to another.

From the above short comparison, it is openly evident that quail farming should be more profitable and less labor and capital intensive, when compared to chicken farming. The benefits of quail farming surpass those of chicken farming in almost all the aspects compared.

You can never go wrong out of an investment in quail farming. All you need is a good preparation before you start to ensure you start the venture on a right track.

How to start quail farming on the right track

'The first step towards success is taken when you refuse to be captive of the environment which you find yourself.'

Mark Caine

Many people venture into certain businesses out of success stories they have heard or witnessed from people who are in similar businesses. Shockingly, a number of people are usually met with frustrations and failures when they set out to carry out such similar businesses on their own. Part of that failure is usually, largely attributed to lack of clear set out goals they intend to achieve.

In order to maximize returns and reap more profits out of quail farming, it is advisable to first put in place a clear quail farming plan. Such a plan should clearly capture all the series of events a quail farmer would be required to undertake before, during and after starting quail farming.

The benefits of having the correct quail raising plan prior to starting out can never be overemphasized. It is what will lead a serious quail farmer towards a more sustainable and profitable undertaking.

A typical quail farming plan should hand to the farmer an opportunity to be able to determine his / her:

- Purpose for production
- Breeding needs.
- Health needs.
- Feeding needs.
- Housing needs.
- Marketing needs. Etc.

Having a correct quail farming plan is the first positive step towards starting quail farming on a right track. It is at the core of becoming and remaining profitable in the quail farming venture.

But with or without the plan, below are some of the basic

essentials necessary for anyone to engage in a profitable quail rearing:

- Being in possession of relevant and up-to-date information on raising the birds. Know what you are getting into and how best you will profitably stay in it.

- Having the right quail breeds from the start, depending on your purpose for rearing the birds: for domestic gains or for commercial purpose. Always remember that *if you start with undesirable breed, their output will be undesirable too, but if you start with a desirable breed, then their output will be desirable.*

- Having the correct housing facility, secure space for raising the quails, depending on your purpose for rearing the birds.

- Having the correct information/knowledge on quail feeds and disease management. In cases where you may be disadvantaged with such information/knowledge, it is advisable to seek for the services of experienced quail/poultry professionals.

- Having adequate latest relevant information on quail farming industry plus market trends.

There can never be enough information on better ways of starting out quail farming, and subsequent management of quail farms. Day in day out, new information and technologies emerge that may help improve on the quality of rearing the birds. It would be of great benefit to look out for such vital information, which would suit your quail farming need. Read relevant materials on quails, from newspapers, magazines, journals, books, websites, blogs etc.

Five qualities of successful quail farmers

'You can never climb the ladder of success with both of your hands in your pockets'.

Anonymous

There are many people who have ventured into quail farming activity across the globe, however, only a few are able to realize profitable returns out of their hard earned investments. And why would it be so? It's because the few successful quail farmers have committed themselves to raising the birds in the correct way. They have chosen to walk the less travelled path, and even gone an extra mile along that infamous route.

Have a look at the five most common qualities that have been exhibited by a group of these successful quail farmers.

Note: I compiled this list out of careful observation of some of the few successful quail bird farmers I interacted with before writing this material.

First quality: Daring and open minded

Truth be told, quail farming or any other poultry related venture isn't a thing for the faint at heart. Most successful quail farmers are willing, more than a hundred percent, to fail and will never stop trying again until they get it right. They have a daring spirit and aren't scared of taking risks. However, they usually take calculated risks in their undertakings. Anyway, *if you don't buy a ticket, you can never win any lottery.*

They are open minded to new ways and ideas that might help them improve on the day to day management of their farms. They are always on continued pursuit for the next best practices and technologies that might help them to manage their farms better. Nothing can ever stop them from investing, heavily, on such new and relevant technologies, i.e. on new brooders, new cages, improved feeds, etc.

When called upon, they are ever ready to attend relevant quail farming events and other farmer related forums. They are thirsty for more information and other better ways of running their farms.

Second quality: Pro-active and very passionate

Nothing good can be realized on a silver platter. Hard work that's hidden in ones passion in any given activity is what eventually translates into good returns in any business venture. Most successful quail farmers are aware of this golden secret and use it to their advantage.

They are ready to seek for help in areas that they are least knowledgeable about, regarding relevant aspects of raising quails. In equal measure, they are more than willing to share such and any other relevant information they might be having, regarding quail farming with other farmers.

They are very passionate in the way they run their farms. This passion brings a long focus and commitment in their undertakings, which eventually translates into positive returns out of their quail rearing.

They are thirsty for more relevant information, and undying ability to read comprehensively from relevant sources i.e. relevant newspapers, journals, magazines, blogs etc. They do this to help them gather varied information available which might help them to manage their farms better.

Third quality: They are always patient

Successful quail farmers are always patient, even against a backdrop of tangible farm related disasters. When misfortunes come calling i.e. massive deaths of their quail chicks due to extreme weather conditions or due to other unexplainable circumstances, they are always patient and would readily move on to bring in and breed more stock.

They patiently feed their birds on correct diet and provide for relevant vaccinations and other necessary farm inputs. They are equally in no rush to market their produce at irrelevant market prices. Significantly, they tend to avoid quick-returns-like related market scenarios. This patience ultimately pays off in the long run.

Fourth quality: They are prayerful and grateful

Successful quail farmers acknowledge the importance of prayer and gratitude. Through prayers, they have learnt how 'to move their mountains'. With lots of humility, they appreciate everyone within their environment. Literally, they don't take anything for granted.

There are those moments in life when they are usually in pursuit of a source of inspiration and strength bigger than theirs, and the only way to draw such inspiration and strength is through prayers. They possess an unwavering faith and trust in their Maker.

Fifth quality: They give back to their societies

Successful quail farmers unreservedly, give back to their societies. They either volunteer their free time and services to local charity based institutions, or they do donate food stuffs or cash to the less fortunate within their societies.

Some of them have even adopted less fortunate children and even sponsored some less privileged students to learning institutions. They always believe in the proverbial 'freely, give more in order to receive more'.

Who are the consumers of quail products?

'If you wait until there is another case study in your industry, you will be too late.'

Seth Godin

In order to establish the best markets and marketing strategies for selling quail products, it is important to understand who the consumers of quail products are. We live in challenging times where each and everyone has their own preferences and tastes out of the many different products or services made available in any given market set up.

Before hurriedly going out in the market and try to sell any quail product to every Dick and Hurry, it is vital for a quail farmer to gain a deeper understanding of his/her prospective consumers. After all, it is the consumers of any given product or service who forms up a market for the same.

When it comes to the consumption of quail products, there are five types of existing consumers that every quail farmer should be aware of.

Number one: The natural consumers

- These are persons who are born and bred in families that consume Quail's products. They have knowledge of quails' products from birth and are always in pursuit of these products for consumption at their homes. In a nut shell, they are simply natural consumers of quails' products.

Number two: The induced consumers

- Induced consumers are people who have been brought up in families who had no access to quails' products, interest or knowledge of quail products, but these people have ended up being introduced into consuming quails' products; either through their close friends, other family members, through quail bird related events and forums, or through other events best known by them.

Equally, part of this group comprises of those people who can easily be lured into consuming quail products due to the nutritional, health and medicinal benefits that have been proven to exist in some of the quails' products like eggs. They may wish to consume quail's products as a prescription to their ailments.

Number three: Induceable consumers

- Just like induced consumers, the induceable consumers are those persons who have been brought up in families or setups where there was no access to quails' products, but they have no challenge being introduced into consuming any quail product. Perhaps, they were brought up in backgrounds that had never tasted any quail product. However, they are willing and ready to start and continue consuming quail products.

This group also contains those people who may get swayed into consuming quails' products due to the nutritional, medicinal, and health benefits found in products such as quail eggs. In a nut shell, it is the induceable consumers who give birth to induced consumers.

Number four: Industrial consumers

These are institutions, organizations and or companies that:

- ❖ Use quail's products as raw materials in processing other consumer related products.

- ❖ Use quail's products to add value to some consumer related products.
- ❖ Imports quail's products for uses better known to them, i.e. to add value, repackage, and send back to the same markets, or send to poverty stricken areas in form of food aids.

Number five: Non-consumers

- There are people who have never tasted any quail product and have no intention of doing so in any future; near of far. This may be as a result of their strict religious backgrounds, health conditions, or due to other factors better explained by such individuals.

  Equally, this group may contain those who are strict vegetarians, or those who are allergic to consuming any form of meat or eggs.

In summary: Any production of any quail's product should be geared towards meeting the consumptions needs of natural consumers, induced consumers, induceable consumers and industrial consumers. However, before jumping into the various markets and marketing strategies that quail farmers can rely on, let's first understand some of the general reasons why anyone would want to buy any product or service from any given market. Why do consumers buy what they buy?

Six reasons why consumers buy what they buy

'The aim of marketing is to know and understand the customer so well the product or service fits him and sells itself.'

Peter Drucker

The ultimate goal of any produced product is for it to reach its intended market, and finally, to its consumer. The real work therefore, lies in the identification of these specific consumers and making them aware of the availability of products they might be interested in

It is important to understand some of the major reasons why consumers buy certain goods and services. Therefore, let me show you the top six reasons why any consumer would spend his/her hard earned cash on any given product or service. Hopefully, these reasons may help any upcoming quail farmer in making relevant preparations while attempting to approach different market segments.

Reason number one: They have a need and there exists a product or service in the market that meets that need

This is the top reason why most people buy what they buy. Anyone who wants to purchase a nice cloth would be headed to a store selling such clothes. It would be hard to find someone looking for a cloth in a food restaurant; not unless the food restaurant has a segment dealing with clothes.

Consumers do not necessarily care about specific people selling certain goods or services. They are concerned with the specific products that they are after. They more often go after products or services that meet their specific needs, save for countable cases of impulse buying.

Reason number two: They are in pursuit of value for their money

A number of people today are very sensitive and cautious on how they spend their hard earned money. On top of most shopping lists today is demand for value of money spent. Notably, it is in the consumers' feedback that anyone selling any product would establish if such a product is of any useful value to clients. However pricey a product might seem, if its value matches its price, then such a product would be consumers' favorite.

You are always the first customer to any product or service you are selling. If you were to purchase it at that given price, would you get value for your money? This is one question you should always ask yourself before going out to sell that product/service. Should you establish that the product would not offer you value at that price, then that's the same feeling the product would receive from its intended clients, and may even lead to loss of your valuable customers.

Reason number three: Out of good recommendation from satisfied clients

A good product recommendation from a satisfied consumer may bring in more sales and sales leads, more than a paid up advertisement in any given local media. That's how powerful positive customer reviews and recommendations are. In the long run, such good recommendations usually end up luring a number of undecided clients to eventually make up their minds and purchase products/services under focus.

Interestingly, there are instances where certain clients have reported purchasing of products/services that they never had urgent any need of, out of some good recommendation from close friends or relatives.

Reason number four: Convenient products

An anonymous best put it that *today, we live in a microwave-like society*. And truth is, most people world over are in need of products that are more convenient to use, and would readily purchase such products. A typical example in the poultry segment is the availability of already prepared chicken's meat, ready for consumption, in most supermarket shelves. Most people are never interested in the deep rooted processes of products that they purchase. They are simply on the look for the ready-to-use products. If we continue with the same example above, there are consumers who are comfortable purchasing a live chicken and would happily proceed home to go complete the whole process of making a meal out of it. But notably, there is a growing portion of the current population who feels uncomfortable with all the details of converting a live chicken into a meal, and would readily purchase a partially prepared chicken's meat, or a fully prepared chicken's meat for consumption.

It is therefore very vital for any quail farmers to know in advance the most convenient products that better suits their varied market demands. Such convenient products would help their consumers to save on time.

Reason number five: Freebies

Who doesn't love free gifts…. especially if the freebies are given out in good faith? However, most consumers aren't necessarily looking out for free goods/ services. They are in pursuit of products and services that might help them save a few coins.

Whenever you get an opportunity to be present at local farming exhibitions, you should turn such events into opportunities for connecting with lots of consumers, by offering some of your quail's products i.e. eggs at prices below your everyday prices. Consumers will find it hard to ever forget such kind gestures and you may be surprised to pull a good number of them from your competition.

Reason number six: Credible and reliable products

Almost all consumers are looking out for credible and reliable products. In a world filled with counterfeit products, consumers usually embrace new products with lots of reservations. They want some assurance that the products they are purchasing are reliable enough to live their intended purposes. Occasionally, they may make a few purchases in order to allow them go and try out any new products; and may never again re-surface to make any future purchases should such products fail to meet their expectations. Anyway, the customer is always right.

When translated to quail farming, there are instances where some farmers have been reported to use certain non-conventional medicines to raise certain breeds of quails. Consuming such birds may pose health risks to consumers and in most instances, the use of such non conventional drugs specifically for raising broilers often results into a tasteless broilers' meat. This could make a quail farmer to a good number of valuable due to negative customer complains.

Markets and marketing strategies

'Transforming a brand into a socially responsible leader doesn't happen overnight by simply writing new marketing and advertising strategies. It takes effort to identify a vision that your customers will find credible and aligned with their values.'

Simon Mainwaring

It takes time, discipline and patience for any serious individual to be able to extract gainful returns out of any business venture.

The main challenge faced by a majority of quail farmers is the crazy idea of trying to sell all their products to the same market, using similar strategies. Automatically, pricing becomes a major issue. The lower the prices, the higher the chances of making sales. Shockingly, even making that sale becomes a matter of probability. It's never guaranteed.

Let's play a scenario where in a given area, all quail farmers are just focusing on one market say, a one supermarket, to sell all their products to. What would happen in the long run? Eventually, there would be an oversupply of quail products in that supermarket; at unrealistically low prices (every one of them would be trying to at least make a sale from that supermarket). This would finally lead to desperate acts by a number of the farmers and eventually lead to deaths of their dreams. So many would be successful quail farmers have given up because of what they term as lack of lucrative markets.

The greatest secret to a more lucrative quail farming venture is for any serious farmer to venture out and possibly create a market of their own.

Below are markets and marketing strategies any quail farmer can employ in order to yield good returns out of their quail farming investments.

Join quail farming/poultry farming related social groups

There are lots of quail farming social groups that are on various social media platforms such as Facebook linked in, twitter, blogs, websites etc. Start out by joining the quail farming social groups whose focus is within your region. Thereafter, you can join the International ones.

Through such social forums, a quail farmer has a valuable opportunity to meet fellow farmers who may either be looking for quail related products, or may be just sharing out their vital farming experiences with the rest of members in that group. Through joining such groups, a farmer has the unlimited room to learn more about quail farming from other's similar experiences. It is a forum for soliciting firsthand farm experiences of other farmers, as they freely share or even ask questions regarding quail farming.

Such social groups have provided avenues for most quail farmers to make that very first important sale. And it is in the making of that initial sale that any quail farmer would get the motivation to improve on his/her farm, and make relevant improvements for more sales in the future.

Export markets

Finding a viable export market is every quail farmer's nightmare. Almost every commercial quail farmer I have interacted with has this strong desire to export their products in exchange for the lucrative foreign currencies. However, most of them dream of exporting larger quantities that they do not even posses in the first place.

Most quail farmers cannot reliably satisfy the demand of quails' products within their regions of operations. The untapped markets and potentials within their countries are still green, and until they are able to fully satisfy the demands from their local markets, they should never shift their focus to want to export the birds' products to other countries.

China has for a long time been a major export destination for quail products. This has been due to the broad Chinese unique cuisine, the country's high population and unending innovative ways of utilizing quails' products in several industries. However, the main question is: how can anyone identify the specific institutions or companies that may want to import quail products?

We live in interesting times where any information is now almost freely available over the internet. These are no periods of compiling a specific list of companies dealing in certain specific products and keeping it safe somewhere. From my personal experience, the best way to locate or identify a viable export markets is through the use of internet. Why would I advocate for use of internet over any other medium? It's because, most companies today have an online presence. Therefore, it is easy to identify and locate specific companies or institutions that may be in need of quails' products through use of internet. You need to take time and search for any relevant export market information on any quail product you intend to export, and in flash, all relevant feedbacks will pop out for you to choose from.

I honestly believe that the use of internet is one of the most current and a relevant way to locate viable export markets for quails' products. Theoretically, this may sound unfulfilling, but practically, it is worth the effort. However, always take note not to fall into the wrong hands of online fraudsters. Always ask around and verify the authenticity of your export target before you officially engage them.

Engage services of a sales or marketing professional

If you have doubts in your sales and marketing capabilities, or want help in making a good number of sales per given period of time, you can employ services of someone else: a professional in sales and marketing.

You should only engage services of such persons if you have adequate stock/supply of quail products, and be willing to adequately compensate the person, based on the job specifications / agreements, or on targets set and met. Out of a personal experience, the best way to work with any sales professional is to agree on certain targets. There is a sales rule that *figures don't lie*.

Supply to local supermarkets

Selling quail products to local supermarkets is every quail farmer's dream idea. This is because of the many customers who shop in such places. It is therefore, a guarantee that any product stocked in any supermarket has to be seen by clients, and may possibly be sold at the end of the day.

Truth be told, supermarkets can be lucrative venues for selling quail products, if and only if fewer farmers make available their quail related products to such stores. However, if many farmers avail their products for sale, then it might not be all that lucrative. There may be a scenario of too much supply that out-meets clients' needs, hence resulting into lowering of prices to attract more sales and to create more room for addition of new stock.

Quail products intended for sale in supermarkets should be neatly packed and clearly labeled. This is a direct way of acquiring more sales and sales leads, and may expose a quail farmer to more sales opportunities.

Reach out to food nutritionists

Due to quail's meat being a favorite alternative source of white meat, the demand for the meat plus the eggs has continued to register an increase in demand from an increasing number of food nutritionists. Your task is therefore, to compile an up-to-date list of nutritionists in your area, and inquire from them if they could be in need of any quail product.

One beautiful thing about working with nutritionists is that they are usually attached/linked to certain organizations or institutions. If you are successful, then you may get links to these institutions and subsequently have your kill.

Supply to specific individual households

Due to the continued recommendation of white meat over red meat by health experts, most nutrition savvy households are best positioned as reliable customers for quail products.

There are many families world over, where a breakfast without an egg is regarded as no breakfast. If there are such families nearby, and even others who may be frequent or even infrequent consumers of quail products, then try to reach out to them. Stay alert and establish as many contacts as you can.

Supply to hospitals and other government/private institutions

As an alternative source of white meat and protein, most hospitals readily recommends for the consumption of quail meat by their ailing patients, over the common red meat. Any serious quail farmer should find avenues of partnering with such nutrition savvy hospitals in order to make available quail products, should they be in need of any.

Equally, a number of government institutions are usually in great demand of quail products, to be consumed during breakfasts, lunch breaks and any other time they congregate for meetings / conferences. Any deal/contract secured by a farmer to supply quail products to such government/private institutions is usually rewarding.

Introduction to local markets

Start selling quail products in local markets, especially in close areas/local markets around where you stay. It is often said that good things are usually nurtured at home. Then slowly, expand to other markets within the same region. And finally you can reach the rest of the markets in the entire country, and across the globe. Start small but dream big.

Supply to local/International non-governmental organizations

There are several local and international non-governmental organizations working in drought prone areas. Equally, there are other Ngo's whose missions are nutrition based. These and other similar Ngo's are usually the biggest consumers of quail products. Get in touch with such organizations.

Be present in relevant agricultural exhibitions

Try to find a space/a stand whenever there are local relevant agricultural exhibitions i.e. during local agricultural shows, agricultural related exhibitions, or any other form of event that might attract the interest of consumers of quail products.

Being present in such events will help you build more useful contacts and even to generate more sales and sales leads. Many successful quail farmers have benefitted a lot from being present in such similar exhibitions. Do not be left behind.

Be ready to offer free samples

Whenever your neighbors, friends and relatives pay you a visit, give them a few samples of the products from your quail farm. Next time, some of these people will turn out to be your life time supporters in form of clients.

There is a golden sales rule *that people often would buy first from people they know or trust*. What you are doing by giving out free samples is building on that trust with clients. And the end result will be to gain the trust and favorability of these clients. Should they be in need of quail related products, you will be the first person they contact.

Supply to various institutions of learning

There are endless lists of persons who have become millionaires out of quail farming, and due to the continued more positive economic impact of quail farming across the globe, several institutions of learning have continued to be in demand for a variety of quail birds, plus quail products for: breeding purposes, learning purposes, and for consumption. Look out for such institutions and tap into their demand stream.

Be an effective ambassador of your brand

Give out your quail farming testimony to your friends and relatives. Equally, willingly mentor or guide other upcoming quail farmers, or people interested in quail farming. You never know when the gods of good luck might pay you a visit and reward you for your efforts.

Write emails, text your friends, create a website, develop a catchy and convincing sales pitch to help you eliminate any sales resistance and position you ahead of other quail farmers. Aim to make your brand visible within your region. Look out for occasions like church functions, networking forums, group meetings and any other relevant event which might attract the attendance of consumers of quail products.

Woo customers from the competition

We live in an era where customers are in unending pursuit of quality products and services from reliable and credible persons/institutions. Use freebies to lure consumers from your competition and find ways of retaining them for a longer duration, should they cross over.

Know what the competition is offering and try to outsmart their offer. Equally, generate as many positive feedbacks from your satisfied clients as you can, in order to use the same in and attracting and retaining new consumers from your competition.

Keep and reward your current customers and find avenues of making them remain loyal for life

Be creative and think outside the box. Find attractive ways of recruiting new customers while at the same time, retaining the existing ones. Any profitable business enterprise depends on the loyalty of its clients. If you must reward your clients in order to maintain their loyalty, then never hesitate to do so. But reward them calculatively, so that you do not run into any debt or even close shop due to losses.

The two most common misconceptions about quail farming

'Real success is that small voice which urges you on against a backdrop of an almost tangible failure.'

Francis Otieno

That domesticated quail birds have no health, medicinal, and nutritional values.

I have personally read and heard some comments from close friends and associates insinuating that feeding domesticated quail birds on commercial feeds makes them loose their much hyped nutritional, health and medicinal values. That, it is only the quail birds in the wild which do posses those nutritional, medicinal, and health values due to the nature of unique feeds they eat in the wild.

This is a misconception. Eating commercial feeds does not make any quail bird lesser of other quail birds. Eating commercial feeds doesn't convert any quail bird into another bird. They still remain quail birds which lay nutritious eggs and provide delicious meat with proven health and medicinal benefits.

That quail farming is a pyramid scheme

When I first heard about quail farming being equated to a pyramid scheme, I went into an uncontrolled laughter. Honestly, I could not imagine that a section of our society had sunk that low, to the extent that they now view any viable agribusiness venture via the lenses of a pyramid scheme. According to Wikipedia.com, a pyramid scheme is defined as *an unsustainable business model that involves promising participants payment or services, primarily for enrolling other people into the scheme, rather than supplying any real investment or sale of products or services to the public.*

Even from that simple definition, it beats any viable logic trying to go into details and want to explain to anyone that quail farming can never be anything close to a pyramid scheme. It is therefore very disheartening, to find a section of quail farmers who want to believe in such ignorant statements. One then is only left to wonder whether such farmers are into quail farming for quick returns, or they are into it to offer consumers value for their money!

'Don't be afraid to get creative and experiment with your marketing.'

Mike Volpe

Other Books By The Author

- **Quail Farming For Beginners**: A quick a to z beginners guide on raising healthy quails

- **Quails 101**: The most asked questions and answers on quail farming

- **Quail Diseases**: Causes, preventions and cure

THE END